The Real-Life Story of Crazy Ralph

The Real-Life Story of Crazy Ralph

HIS GRANDEST ADVENTURE CAN NEVER BE TOPPED. NEVER.

STORY BY **BOPPA HARMON**
ILLUSTRATIONS BY DMITRY GITELMAN

The Real-Life Story of Crazy Ralph

Copyright © 2025 Paul Harmon

All rights reserved. No part of this publication may be reproduced, distributed, or transmitted in any form or by any means, including photocopying, recording, or other electronic or mechanical methods, or for any purposes, including artificial intelligence technology usages, without the express prior written permission of the publisher, except in the case of brief quotations embodied in critical reviews and certain other noncommercial uses permitted by copyright law.

ISBN 979-8-218-66425-1
Library of Congress Control Number 2025907845

Illustrations by Dmitry Gitelman
Cover and Book Design by Paul Nylander | Illustrada

Published by Paul Harmon
Saint Paul, Minnesota

Contents

Foreword   vii

1.	What in the world is this place?	1
2.	The adventuring kickoff!	5
3.	Where's my mother? What's going on?	9
4.	The totally unexpected opportunity—BREAKOUT!	15
5.	What a wonderful world this is!	19
6.	Something's up!	25
7.	Holy Moly, who are all these humans?	29
8.	A born escape artist	35
9.	What does "Merry Christmas" mean? What's a "Present?"	37
10.	It's the simple things	45
11.	Ralph grows into "Crazy Ralph"	49
12.	Runs like a deer, climbs like a squirrel	55
13.	I can fly!	61
14.	Daring escapes—how did he do it?	65

15. Ralph becomes a police dog—briefly	69
16. Look what I found, Dad! Can I keep him . . . please, pleeease?	73
17. Can you take the little guy in? Would it be OK with Ralph?	77
18. Get outa my way, you big fur bag!	83
19. Double trouble	89
20. Two years of living crammed into each year of life	93
21. It all came on unexpectedly	99
22. The adventure of all adventures! The grandest of them all!!	103
Epilogue	115
Dedication	119
Acknowledgments	121

Foreword

This is a true story. Parts may be quite hard to believe. That's what makes it "crazy"—all the outrageous over-the-top things that teeter on the very edge of believability. And all because of Ralph later to be joined by his little buddy, Squirt. Just what made Ralph like he was will forever remain a mystery. Full of joy and love and mischievous adventure. Almost like a cartoon character. But every bit as real as you and I. And what he was said to have done and how he did it are as real and accurate as memories can recall. His greatest adventure was—and is to this day—literally out of this world. It can never be topped. Never. But it can be equaled. You'll see.

Get ready to step inside the world of non-stop discovery, adventuring and wild "get-outa-my-way" fun. You're stepping into Ralph's world. And you can believe it, Ralph would've loved to have had you by his side.

CHAPTER 1
What in the world is this place?

It was November 2000. A long time ago now. A rather chubby, black female dog was having trouble. She would pace from side to side, yelping now and then. As days went by her yelps became more frequent and louder. She was taken to the veterinarian to find out what was troubling her.

"Just as I thought, she's pregnant," the vet announced, "she has little puppies growing inside her." And the yelping? What was causing that? Probably one or more of the puppies was kicking. And a little harder, it seemed, as the days went by and the itty-bitty puppies grew larger. The vet said she'd never seen such big kicks and so frequent.

The kicks moved towards the center of the soon-to-be mother's tummy, then down a little later, then back up again. Odd. Very odd. It seemed that it was the same puppy doing the kicking. Somebody wanted out. He or she continued moving back and forth, up and down, as the days went by. And Mother just kept on yelping quietly, then wagging her tail. The kicks weren't hurting her. They just seemed to startle her.

Soon it was time . . . time for the puppies to come out into the world. There were 6 altogether. Each came out into the world wiggling and squirming. And each was hungry and searching for mother's milk and wanting to cuddle next to her warm tummy.

Except for one. A male puppy had, evidently, elbowed his way to the front of the line to be the first to get out from inside his mother. He was already crawling. And he seemed to be more interested in exploring the world than having a meal of mother's warm milk like the other puppies.

First, he crawled under his mother's leg as she lay on her side, then he tried to climb up her. Unstable, he fell over backward. But he quickly righted himself and started climbing up his mother's back again. His little paws never stopped moving, it seemed. Could this be the kicker . . . the puppy that was startling his mother with his "fist bumps" (guess we should say, "paw bumps") day after day after day?

He was the smallest of his brothers and sisters which is often referred to as the "runt of the litter." And oh so handsome. Pitch black like the others except for his brilliant white markings. The top of his paws looked like they were covered in sparkling white snow. A large patch running down the front of his little chest was also brilliant white fur. Last, the tip of his little tail looked like it was dipped in bright white paint.

The runt had the cutest little face that anyone had ever seen! You couldn't help but notice how handsome he was

What in the world is this place?

. . . that is if he'd stop long enough to let you get a good look at him.

Now puppies are born blind and deaf. And they stay that way until they're around 2 weeks old. They don't even open their eyes until then. So puppies rely on their sense of smell to find their mother. But the little "runt" with white paws and a splash of white on his chest and that cute little white-tipped tail didn't seem to care that he couldn't see or hear. He was intent on exploring his new world. And his nose worked just fine.

The little runt of the litter was like a Bumper Car at a carnival. When he bumped into something—a brother or sister or a nearby wall—he just abruptly turned around and kept exploring. His little legs, not even 2 inches long, seemed to be in non-stop motion. He was obviously on an adventure to find out everything he could about the world and to experience all that it had to offer. No one knew it then but they were witnessing the beginning of what could only be called a "grand adventure."

That grand adventure began in a way that nobody could have ever predicted.

CHAPTER 2
The adventuring kickoff!

It shouldn't have been a surprise, it was later said, that the little guy started to open his eyes when he was only 10 days old . . . a full 4 days earlier than his brothers and sisters. And his ears began to hear things, too. It probably shouldn't have been a surprise either that he almost immediately started running as fast as his stubby little legs could carry him. Actually, it wasn't running. It was more like a fast waddle as he swayed from side to side trying to keep his balance, tipping over quite frequently.

    He was so eager to explore his new world that he would just charge into whatever was around him . . . the leg of a chair, a cabinet door, a brother or sister. Made no difference what it was. He immediately sniffed it, licked it and rubbed it with his short little snout. Every odor was new and exciting. Every lick of his tongue was a new taste experience. Every rub of his snout against something was a new feeling, a new texture. Every sound was exciting and helped to paint a more complete

The Real-Life Story of Crazy Ralph

picture of his surroundings. The little runt couldn't get enough of this world he'd just stepped into.

And now as his eyes were beginning to work, although presenting rather blurry images to the little fella, he began to understand what seeing was all about. What a wonderful thing! The smells from his nose, the tastes from his tongue, the feels from his snout-rubs, the surrounding sounds from his ears. And now a picture to go with it. Wow! You could see how he felt just by looking at his face: "I absolutely love this world!"

And then it happened. The "adventuring kickoff." A new sensation that the little fast-waddling pup had never experienced before. You see, right next to where he stayed with his mother and brothers and sisters, there was a swinging door that a human would occasionally push open and walk through. Then the door would quickly (and powerfully, as the little fella would soon learn) swing back to close. He had timed the door swing so, when it opened, he could sneak through before anyone noticed and see what exciting things were on the other side. He timed his move to get through the door during the few moments it was swung open. Off he went at just the right moment as the door opened. BUT he didn't take into account what would happen when the door swung shut . . . with his tiny butt in just the right place to be booted across the room. It was like a baseball player hitting the ball with a bat. Only this ball was a furry little white-pawed runt and the bat was a swinging door!

The door swung back. Fast. First, the hard "whop" on the runt's butt. Then the hit on his head as the door swept him into

The adventuring kickoff!

the railing posts lining the downstairs steps. Next, he bounced off the post and down the stairs. Head over butt, head over butt, head over butt. Finally, he landed on the hardwood floor at the bottom of the stairs—the final head over butt.

Yes, it hurt. A lot. The little fearless runt of an explorer had just experienced pain for the first time. Now you would think that this would discourage him from further explorations. Or at least make him a little more cautious. Nope. Not at all. To the little guy, pain was simply another experience, another new sensation. It was all part of fully embracing his new world. And indeed, this acceptance of all sensations—bitter tastes, sweet tastes, good smells, nasty smells and, yes, even occasional pain—was the stuff that adventures were made of. And from this day on and for the rest of his life, the little white-pawed runt would always be on an adventure. Every day, every place, every thing. Always a new adventure. This adventure-seeking is what God put inside him. And it would never leave him. To the lovable little runt, life was—and would always be—just one big adventure after the other.

CHAPTER 3

Where's my mother? What's going on?

Late one day when the puppies were about 6 weeks old, sometime in mid-December, 2000, they were placed in a soft-sided kennel with a carrying handle on top and a big fluffy blanket lining the bottom. It was the blanket they had all laid on with their mother since they were born. And it smelled so good—just like Mother.

The pups could see out through the plastic mesh screen on the kennel sides but there was no way to get out. That was always the first thought in the little runt's mind no matter where he was: "How do I get out of here?"

The kennel with its full load of pups was put into the back of a car and driven off. It was now dark outside and the pups couldn't see anything. Their mother stayed back.

It was all a little scary. After all, the little puppies had never been anyplace other than the same room in the house where they were born. And only the little runt had even been out of that one room. But what was most unsettling, their mother had always been with them. Until today. Every day, every hour, every minute. She was so soft and warm. It always felt so good to sleep next to her. Now they were alone, all packed in a kennel and being carted off to who knows where.

The experience of a car ride was exciting in a way. They had never been jostled around before—up and down, side to side—as they rode along in this strange contraption. It almost felt like they were in their house but it was bumping around here and there, occasionally jerking to a stop then quickly charging on again. Strange. The little runt liked it. Another new sensation, another new feeling. It made him feel a little queasy—his tummy was a little upset. That was OK though. It too, was just part of the new car-riding experience.

But another feeling that he'd never experienced before had crept into him and wouldn't seem to leave . . . a feeling that would visit him every now and then for the rest of his life. Sadness. A kind of loneliness that kept him from fully enjoying the ride. It was his mother. He missed her. He felt lost. His past adventures always ended with him being tucked into his mother's warm fur with her special scent. It was the smell of, well, safe. He would often crawl up onto her back as she lay just to get a better look around while his brothers and sisters slept beside her. Mother would gently pick him up with her teeth by the thickly furred skin on the back of his neck (called the "scruff"). It didn't hurt, not at all. She would put him down near a "milk station" on her tummy. The milk tasted so good, everything felt so good and smelled so good. There was nothing else like that feeling. Even his mother's warm tummy rising and falling softly as she breathed was special to feel. It kind of gently rocked the little pups to sleep. And now she was gone.

Did I do something wrong? Was it my constant exploring that irritated her? Didn't she want me anymore? When will I see her again? It kept going over and over in his mind, "I want my mother . . . I want my mother . . . I *really* want my mother."

The little runt made a sound that he'd never made before. He wasn't trying. It just came out. It was a soft whine, like a whimper, trailing off into silence. He was crying. He finally drifted off to sleep, deeper and deeper, dreaming that he was cuddled next to his mother . . . all warm and cozy and safe.

Just then the car came to an abrupt halt. The little runt and his siblings were startled awake. The car had bumped into the concrete curb in front of a brick building with a big steel door. The soft-sided kennel with its special cargo of now wide-awake, wiggling puppies was carried inside through the steel door. The puppies were removed from the soft-sided kennel and put into a small space with a thick steel fence—a chain link fence—surrounding it on 3 sides. The back of this space was made of concrete blocks. Actually, the walls of the whole building were concrete blocks. And there were at least a dozen little rooms like theirs along the concrete-block walls. They were, in fact, cages . . . also called kennels. All of the other kennels already had a dog living in them.

Before the puppies were put into their space—that is, their new kennel—their blanket was taken out of the soft-sided kennel they came in, fluffed up, and laid out on their new kennel's floor. It was the same blanket that they had lived on with their mother since they were born. The puppies all scrambled to lay on it again. Like their little white-pawed brother, they too craved the scent of their mother and the blanket was the only comfort any of them now had. They were all alone. Together, yes, but all alone.

That first night in this strange place called an "animal shelter" was hard. The little runt began to whimper softly again. Pretty soon, all 6 puppies were whimpering, each sounding a little different, but yet all sounding of the same sadness. They all missed their mother. The man that was watching over this animal shelter would give them water and some strange food once in a while—and even give them each a quick pat on the head—but none of this was of much comfort.

There was an old, tired-looking Golden Retriever in the kennel next to them. He barely moved. Looked ancient. He hardly noticed when the little runt went to the chain link fence that separated them to say hello. Maybe he was sick?

The black Cocker Spaniel housed in the kennel on the other side of them wasn't much better off. He'd pace in his kennel, back & forth, back & forth. He didn't have much interest in meeting the little runt either. In fact, he didn't seem to have much interest in anything other than pacing back & forth.

The next morning the little white-pawed, ever-adventuresome runt sat straight up with a start. He had a thought. A powerful, I-gotta-do-it thought: "I'm going to get us out of here. I'm going to do whatever it takes to make this place nothing but a rough patch in our history. We'll all leave it behind us."

He started to explore the fenced kennel they were in—that meant inspecting every crack in the block wall that was the back of their kennel, every crevice in the concrete floor they laid on, every bend in the chain link fencing surrounding them. His brothers and sisters slept almost continuously on their mother-scented blanket. But the little runt never stopped moving. Never stopped thinking. He would find a way to get out. A way to get them all out. His little legs seemed to move at the same pace that his thoughts were moving. He couldn't help it. And the more excited he got about breaking out, the faster he'd think and the faster his little legs would move him around the kennel. He watched for every opportunity to make his move.

But something strange was about to happen.

CHAPTER 4

The totally unexpected opportunity— BREAKOUT!

It was that very morning when the little runt made his vow to break out through that big steel outer door. He would wait until it was opened wide. He'd had an encounter with a door before: the swinging door that once booted him down the stairs.

Suddenly, a lady with a rope in her hand walked in. Hmmmm. Who was she? What was she going to do with that rope?

The little runt stared intently at the lady as she opened the kennel door next to them where the big Golden Retriever was staying. She hooked the rope onto the big Retriever, then led him to the steel door and out they went.

When they came back, about 15 minutes later, the old Retriever was all excited and bouncing around like a big furry rubber ball. Turns out, the lady just took him outside for a walk around . . . smelling things, pawing at earthworms, chasing

The Real-Life Story of Crazy Ralph

butterflies, who knows just what was out there or what they did. But that trip through the big steel door filled that old Retriever full of life again. Just a simple walk outside was all it took to turn that old sour puss, she called him Lightning, into the most jubilant fella in the building.

The little runt couldn't help but laugh to himself, "Lightning, what a name for a dog that moved in ultra-slow motion." Ol' Lightning barely shuffled around in his kennel, if he moved at all, the whole time that the little runt had been studying him. "'Sleepy' would be a more fitting name," the runt thought.

The lady put the old Golden Retriever back in his kennel, removed the rope from what she called his collar, gave him some kind of treat and gently patted his head as she softly said, "You're such a good boy, Lightning." The old fella was thoroughly worn out. But ever so happy. Lightning promptly fell asleep with the most content look on his face.

The lady then opened up the kennel door on the other side of the little runt's kennel and took the Cocker Spaniel out for a walk. Maybe a run? And the same thing happened. Dull dog out, happy dog back.

The Cocker Spaniel came prancing back into his kennel—his eyes big and bright and filled with life. "You're so fun to be with, Happy! I can't wait to go for a walk with you again," she said.

"Happy??? Did I hear that right? Did she call him Happy?" the little runt thought to himself, "That furry black critter is anything but happy, pacing mindlessly back and forth in his kennel all day. He should've been named 'In-A-Daze' or maybe 'Trance.'"

The totally unexpected opportunity—BREAKOUT!

The lady repeated the process with all the dogs in the building, sometimes two at a time, until the whole place was alive and excited. Every dog in the building had been out for a walk. Except for the little runt and his siblings.

Outside is the place to be, the runt thought. And he became all the more committed to breaking out soon. He wondered why Lightning and Happy were in this place. Is this where they've lived all their lives? Just the thought of that strengthened the little runt's resolve to break out . . . somehow. He couldn't even let himself think what it would be like to live his life in this prison.

The little fella didn't know that Lightning had been brought into the animal shelter just a short time ago because his long-time human dad had to be hospitalized. It was thought that his dad was dying. There was no place else for Lightning to go. The likelihood of Lightning being adopted by a new family wasn't very good. Most everyone, it seems, wants little puppies and Lightning was already over 10 years old.

Happy came to the animal shelter because his human mom & dad had to move from their home into an apartment that didn't allow pets. They were deeply saddened that Happy couldn't come with them. Like Lightning, Happy was old for a dog, 8 ½ years old, so his chances of being adopted weren't much better. And both Lightning and Happy loved their human moms and dads so much that they probably couldn't imagine being with anyone else.

The little runt was lost in his thoughts when the lady startled him by opening HIS kennel door. She was quite

The Real-Life Story of Crazy Ralph

pretty . . . as humans go. She reached into the kennel, picked up each little puppy one at a time, and slowly stroked their furry backs. This was the runt's chance. Just as she reached for another of his brothers, he dodged around her—she wasn't quite fully blocking their kennel door. He made it outside the kennel door and was heading for the big steel door, which she had left slightly ajar, as fast as he could. His little legs were flying.

Just as he reached the slightly opened door . . . "whoosh" . . . the lady scooped him up with one swift swing of her arm and brought him right up to her face. "Where are you going, little one?" she asked. "I bet you'd like to go outside."

Her eyes were warm and kind. Yes, she was pretty . . . on the inside, too . . . which is the only place that "pretty" really counts. The runt had looked into the eyes of every human he'd ever encountered and this lady was the prettiest on the inside that he'd seen. As she ran her hand softly across his back she said, "My name is Debbie. What's yours? Oh, I forget, you don't have a name yet, do you?"

She walked back to his kennel as she held him, then gently placed him inside with a departing promise: "You're really a little young to be going outside yet and it's almost dark now anyway. But it's going to be exceptionally warm for the next few days. I'll come back and we'll go for a big long walk with Mr. Sun on our shoulders . . . soon . . . very soon." And with that, she closed their kennel door and left.

Little did the runt know that this lady who called herself Debbie would turn out to be his ticket to freedom.

CHAPTER 5
What a wonderful world this is!

The next day the lady who called herself Debbie returned. It was a beautiful sunny day. She propped the steel door open slightly to let some fresh air in and, again, took each dog out for a walk . . . one by one, sometimes two at a time.

The little puppies, the runt and his brothers and sisters, were alive with anticipation. Something was going to happen today. They sensed that this was the day they would get to go outside. The runt was certain of it. He could feel it in his bones. He was the first to start yipping at their kennel door and soon all of his sibling puppies were doing the same. "Yip, Yip, Yip." They were very high-pitched "Yips." The puppies were still so small that they really couldn't bark. But they sure did get Debbie's attention.

"O.K., O.K. . . . today is the day but you'll have to wait your turn," she told them as she returned one dog to its kennel and hooked another on the short rope she called a leash. The little

runt could never wait for anything. He just yipped more and louder giving it everything he had. And of course, his brothers and sisters followed suit. They yipped all the more and all the louder, too.

Finally, the lady came to their kennel carrying a large basket with a blanket on the bottom. She swung open their kennel door, loaded them all into the basket, and off they went toward the steel door . . . still yipping but now out of pure excitement.

"C'mon," she said, "you're going to see the great outdoors today." She kept her hand on the runt because he kept trying to climb out of the basket. She could barely hold him down. It was a little cool outside. But this was an unusually warm day and the bright sun made it even warmer.

They all went through the big steel door. They could barely see when they got outside. The light was so bright. They all squinted. This was their first introduction to Mr. Sun. And it took a little time for their eyes to get used to him.

The little runt could barely contain his excitement. His whole body was shaking, more like vibrating. Debbie started to put the basketful of excited puppies down on the ground but the little runt leaped over the side before she could catch him. He landed on the thick green grass. You'd think it would hurt, at least a little. But the runt sure didn't show it if it did. He immediately started to sniff the grass, then taste it, then run in it and roll around in it. It felt so good. The grass, the sun, the warmth, the gentle breeze. Every sensor in his body was drinking it in.

The Real-Life Story of Crazy Ralph

It would take hundreds of pages and thousands of words to explain what all the runt and his little brothers and sisters experienced on their first day outside. The runt was overwhelmed with all the smells and tastes and feelings that he was experiencing. Yes, the outside world was where he wanted to be for all time. It was more than he could ever have imagined—"What a wonderful world this is!"

The runt decided to make a break for it right then and there. He barely made it to the fence that surrounded the grass-covered lot they were in when Debbie grabbed him and loaded him and all the puppies back into the basket and headed toward the big steel door. The runt quickly nipped off a withered, yellow dandelion just as she picked him up. He was busy chewing it as Debbie put all the puppies back in their kennel for the night. They had never experienced such excitement. They'd never been able to run around like that. They were tired to the bone. All fell asleep immediately . . . even the runt with the partially chewed, wilted dandelion dangling out of his mouth. It can be assumed that they all drifted off with dreams of the great outdoors dancing in their heads. They now had memories they'd never had before which they could call on in dreams whenever they wanted.

That night, the runt re-lived every step he'd taken in the great outdoors as he drifted off to sleep . . . every little thing he'd sniffed, every taste, every sound, every feeling of the things he'd touched, and most especially, the wonderful warmth coming from that huge yellow ball high above. And, wow, that enormous and magnificently beautiful blue sky with those puffy white things floating around in it. Even the soft breeze that gently fluffed his fur as it passed by was a treat. "Who in the world made all of these things," he thought. What more was out there for him to experience?

    The runt would soon find out. Sooner than he expected. In fact, it came the very next morning when he awoke.

CHAPTER 6
Something's up!

The little white-chested runt was sleeping soundly after that romp in the wonderful outside world. He was startled awake by two ladies talking in front of his kennel . . . Debbie and a younger girl. Younger, yes, but still a full-size human.

They were pointing at him and his brothers and sisters who had also awakened now. But the brothers and sisters stayed nestled on their blanket, still drowsy and wanting a little more sleep. Not the runt. He was at the kennel door standing on his hind legs, his little white-tipped paws poking through the chain link surrounding their kennel, his short white-tipped tail wagging rapidly back & forth.

Debbie opened their kennel door and, while holding the runt back with one hand so he wouldn't escape, picked up one of his brothers. Debbie handed his brother to the other human, a girl she called Christina. Debbie and Christina talked quietly while the runt jumped up on the chain link fence and ran

The Real-Life Story of Crazy Ralph

around the kennel. He ran right over his brothers and sisters, back and forth, then jumped up on the fence again and again.

Little did anyone know that Christina had come to pick out a puppy to take home with her. Actually, she wasn't going to take a puppy home for herself. The puppy was to be a gift for someone. And Christina wasn't living in a home at all. She lived in a dormitory. That's a place where young people like Christina often live while they go to a school called a university.

Christina stooped down and looked intently at the little runt as she cuddled his brother. The runt tried to sniff her hand as she put it flat on the chain link fence right next to his nose. Then he jumped up & down and danced along the fence on his hind legs. Yes, he was excited.

Debbie, as it turned out, had picked out the runt's brother for Christina. He was more "sedate," she said—meaning he didn't run around and bounce around and dance around and always try to escape like the runt. The runt's brother would, according to Debbie, make a good pet. In fact, any of the runt's siblings would make good pets. The runt, on the other hand, would be difficult for anyone to keep under control. And, having made this clear to Christina, she again advised that she pick any of the other puppies.

Christina pondered her choices looking closely at each brother and sister. They were all so soft and cuddly and cute. The runt was all that and then some, but he never stopped moving. He was always acting a little crazy. Never slowed down. His little legs, in fact, often kept moving even when he was asleep, she was told. The little runt would be hard to take

Something's up!

care of, Debbie again cautioned, as Christina focused on the more "normal" little brother that Debbie had chosen for her . . . and then the others, one by one.

Finally, Christina reached inside the kennel and held the runt back so he couldn't get out while she reached for another puppy. . . at least that's what the runt thought she was doing. But, no, she was reaching for him! She was picking him up!! She closed the kennel door and proudly announced to Debbie, "I want to take this crazy one . . . he's so special."

Having given him time to say goodbye to his siblings, out the big steel door Christina and the little runt went. Which was the beginning of the little, white-pawed pup's life out in the real world. Where was he going to live? Who would he be living with? What in the world is going on? And what does the word "Christmas" mean that Debbie and Christina were talking about?

The answers to all of the runt's questions would be life-changing for him. And they would all be revealed to him soon. Very soon. The answers would all be surprises. Not just to the runt . . . but to everyone. The first surprise came that very day.

CHAPTER 7
Holy Moly, who are all these humans?

Christina drove the little runt to the dormitory where she was living while attending classes at the university. It was the runt's second car ride and it was exciting.

During this ride he was kept in a small, blanket-lined cardboard box from which, as you might expect, he quickly escaped. He spent most of the ride running back and forth in the back seat from one window to another trying to get a peek out.

Pretty soon, he was in the front seat. Then he jumped onto Christina's lap as she drove. At last, from his perch on her lap and with his hind legs fully extended and his front paws on the side window's ledge, he could see outside. He was watching the outside world go by him, trees and roads and grass and bushes and . . . **WHOOOOA** . . . what was that?? Christina noticed that his little eyes were locked on a cow standing in a fenced field but, try as she may, she couldn't properly explain to the runt what he was seeing.

The Real-Life Story of Crazy Ralph

The only thing that dampened the excitement of this "ride of a lifetime," the little fella thought, was that his brothers and sisters weren't with him. He already missed them. And, of course, he still missed his mother. But somehow he knew—absolutely knew—that he would see them all again one day. And it was more than a little comforting to know that Debbie, the "pretty lady on the outside & inside," would be there to watch over his brothers and sisters and find them someone like Christina to take them to a real home. Yup, everyone was safe and he would see them all again one day. In the meantime, he would concentrate on drinking in all these amazing things flying by him outside the car window.

The little guy didn't know it but he had already been given a name that would be his for the rest of his life.

"Meet Ralph!" Christina announced as she held the little runt up for all of the girls she lived with to see. The girls were "pod mates." The "pod" consisted of a group of little rooms in a large building called a dormitory (which is like a huge apartment building).

All five girls had a bed and a closet in this pod. They shared a single bathroom. They also shared an instant love for the cutest little puppy they had ever seen—Ralph. A little black & white "furry dude," they joked. And so cuddly!

The name Ralph, a rather odd name for a dog, was chosen by Christina for a special reason. That reason would become known in a short time. On Christmas morning, to be exact. But we're getting ahead of ourselves.

Ralph set about sniffing his new surroundings. He would barely make it a few steps and one of the girls would pick him up and cuddle him. He liked that. He looked into each of their eyes to see who they were. They all had gentle, loving eyes . . . "Yup, pretty in all the ways that count," he said to himself.

So this was the place he would be living, he thought. Not bad. Not bad at all. Wonderful humans, all kinds of hugs, warm blankets and beds, and the great outdoors that he could see from a big window near Christina's bed. The problem was, though, that the girls all had to attend classes. And it was impossible to leave Ralph alone for even a few minutes. He was always into everything. He never stopped exploring. And yes, he tended to explore thoroughly. He might have to pull a sweater apart to see what it was made of. Or tear open a package of cereal and scatter it all about to see how many pieces were in there. Then eating as many as his little tummy could hold. The bathroom was an especially fun place, what with the warm waterfalls that the humans called a "shower." He liked to sneak into the shower, occupied or not, before anyone could catch him.

His "exploring" during these early days as a puppy was described by some as "ripping everything apart all the time." So he needed someone to constantly watch over him. That wasn't possible with Christina and the other girls having to attend classes. Not only that, school rules did not allow for pets of any kind, including dogs, to stay in their dormitory. It was forbidden. Given the school's strict no-pets rule and Ralph's "explorations" (often quite noisy and most always messy), Christina decided that she must find a safe place to keep him until Christmas, now just a few days away. Ralph didn't know it but Christmas would be the single biggest life-changing event EVER for him. Christmas would be the day that he would be brought to his new home . . . the home where he would live for the rest of his life.

Christina called Debbie, the "pretty inside & outside" dog walker at the kennel, and asked if she would be willing to watch the little runt at her house for a few days. Just temporarily until Christmas. Christina explained that she was afraid that the University's staff would discover Ralph staying in her pod. Moreover, she and her pod mates couldn't properly watch over him. Christina said she would come back to pick him up just before Christmas. "Oh, and by the way," Christina told her, "his name is now Ralph." Debbie readily agreed to take him in for the few remaining days before Christmas. And so that very night Christina brought Ralph to Debbie's house.

Christina arrived at Debbie's and her husband Ed's house with Ralph cradled in her arms . . .and one hand atop his head to keep him from jumping out. Ralph was thrilled to see Debbie again. "I know you!" he thought. "Great to see you again, pretty lady." Ralph wondered if this is where he would be living. Ralph wasn't going to have to wait long to find out.

Debbie had prepared a space just off the kitchen for her furry little guest. Her husband, Ed, put up a wood-framed, plastic-mesh fence to enclose a small area. It was like kennel walls but instead of steel chain links, the links were soft plastic. There was no way to escape. Ralph could then be contained. The temporary kennel certainly would secure him for a few days.

A large, open-top cardboard box was prepared for his bed with soft, comfy blankets lining the bottom for the little runt (now called Ralph) to lay on. It was placed inside the temporary kennel. The box had very high sides so, when they put Ralph to bed for the night, there would be no way for him to get out. And even if by some miracle he did get out of the box, the plastic-mesh fence would contain him in a small part of the house just off the kitchen. Or so Debbie and Ed thought.

Of course, they were quite wrong. Ralph had already become what is sometimes called an "escape artist." And Debbie & Ed would soon be putting his escape skills to the test.

CHAPTER 8
A born escape artist

Debbie put Ralph in his blanket-lined bed inside the tall cardboard box, then she went upstairs to bed. It wasn't 5 minutes before Ralph was out of the cardboard box . . . and but a few minutes more before he had climbed the plastic fence. Or crawled underneath it. It was never determined just how he got out. And so very quickly! The escape-proof kennel that Ed & Debbie had so carefully prepared was no match for Ralph.

Off he was exploring his new surroundings . . . starting in the kitchen near where his "escape-proof" temporary kennel was. This place had some wonderful smells. Food smells of all kinds. His sniffer even found a few morsels just underneath the front of the refrigerator. Then off to the nearby couch to see what it was made of and what it would be like to jump off of and . . .

Just then Debbie swooped him up and brought him back to the cardboard box inside the temporary kennel. She hadn't had enough time to fall asleep before she heard him bumping around downstairs.

Debbie put Ralph back in his box and placed a piece of thick cardboard to cover the top. Then she weighted the cardboard top down with a big, heavy book. Certainly he couldn't get out now, she thought. She whispered softly to Ralph through the slit in the corner of the box, "Now you go to sleep, little one." And up she went to her bedroom again.

Not five minutes later Debbie heard a thud. Yes, that was the book falling off the top of Ralph's box and onto the hardwood floor. Ralph was out again.

And so it went for all 3 days leading up to Christmas that Ralph stayed at Debbie & Ed's house. Ralph would break out, they would further fortify his makeshift kennel, and Ralph would break out again . . . off on another adventure. Truth is, they all were having great fun. Ralph was so cute and so energetic and so cuddly . . . well, you just couldn't get mad at him.

What no one knew at the time was that Ralph's "outings" as a little puppy—that is, his exploring, his adventures, his escapes—were nothing next to what they'd become as he got older. Ralph would later amaze everyone that came to know him with his escapes and other over-the-top adventurous feats. Ralph was in a doggy class all his own.

Then came that life-changing day for Ralph. He was going to yet another house atop a big hill.

CHAPTER 9

What does "Merry Christmas" mean? What's a "Present?"

It was now Christmas eve, December 24th, 2000. A Sunday. Christina came to pick Ralph up from Debbie's house and off they were again. "Guess I won't be living with Debbie and Ed after all," Ralph thought. "They were really nice humans, both pretty on the inside." But it was all part of some grand adventure, he reasoned, and he'd see everyone again soon. Meeting people again always seemed to be the case for little Ralph. So, into the box with a comfy blanket once more. And off he and Christina went.

Ralph had heard the word "Christmas" several times in the last few days but he had no idea what it meant. He had also heard the word "present" a few times but had no idea what that meant, either. He had even heard the two words put together, "Christmas Present." Everything would soon come together for him. It was now Christmas Eve.

What does "Merry Christmas" mean? What's a "Present?"

After a 15-minute car ride from Debbie & Ed's house, Christina and her precious white-pawed cargo arrived at a house with a very steep driveway. Ralph had, as you might have expected, crawled out of his cardboard box. His newly discovered technique was to jump as high as he could on the side wall of the box. Then push with all his weight on the top end of the wall. The box would tip over on its side and Ralph could just walk out. Pretty clever for a little tike with only weeks of living under his furry belt.

After escaping from the box using this "high-jump & push" maneuver and crawling to the front of the car, Ralph perched himself on the very edge of the front passenger seat... straining to see out the side window. As the car lurched forward to climb the steep driveway, Ralph fell over backward. He tumbled to the floor, then quickly scrambled back up to the seat again and leaped onto Christina's lap. Another new experience, he thought, "I'll have to watch out for steep hills when riding in a car."

Ralph didn't know it then but he would be climbing this hill thousands of times for years to come—in cars, trucks, tractors, and almost anything that had wheels. Even boats on their trailers. But, most often, just using his own legs.

The car stopped when it reached the top of the hill. Ralph was gently put back in the box, the top was closed and a "Merry Christmas" card was taped on the top. Oops. Christina almost forgot something. She opened the box up and affixed a little red ribbon on the top of Ralph's head.

Christina and her wiggling box with its special cargo inside went straight into the house, opening the back door lock with her key. You see, she had lived in this house most all of her life and was only living temporarily in the university dormitory with her pod mates. This was her childhood home. The place where she grew up.

She walked straight into the kitchen and, instead of saying "Hello" to her mom and dad who were sitting at the kitchen table, she greeted them with a joyously loud, "Merry Christmas!" Then, without pausing for even a second, she handed the bouncing box to her dad. "Go ahead, open it, open your Christmas present!" she said. Ralph, of course, didn't understand what was going on. Yes, he'd heard the words "Christmas present" before but he didn't know that . . .

. . . HE was the Christmas present!

Yes, Ralph was a Christmas present from Christina to her mom and dad. A living, squirming, fuzzy little ball of deep black fur with brilliant white markings. But why, of all things, a dog for a Christmas present? Well, Christina thought her parents' house was all too quiet after she moved to her college dormitory. Christina was her parents' only child. And when she and her friends weren't around anymore—talking and laughing and playing music and telling jokes—the house became just too quiet. So, Christina reasoned, the house needed to be noisier, cheerier, happier. Simply put, it needed to be livened up. A dog might just do the trick, she thought. She picked Ralph out from the litter at the kennel because he was so "alive" all the time. He never seemed to stop moving. He was always

What does "Merry Christmas" mean? What's a "Present?"

exploring, always on an adventure. He was guaranteed to liven up the house!

Ralph's ribbon-adorned head popped up immediately as Christina's dad opened the box. And, just as immediately, Ralph started to jump out.

Dad was startled. He hadn't expected a living creature inside the carboard box! Mom was startled, too. Taken aback as they were, Ralph was able to get out of the box with one big pull of his front paws on Dad's hands and jumped right onto Dad's lap.

As Ralph popped out of the box and onto Dad's lap, Christina asked, "And you know what his name is?" Not waiting for an answer, Christina loudly proclaimed . . .

"RALPH! His name is RALPH!!"

Christina was overjoyed! Finally, after 22 years of life, it was time for payback!! You see, when Christina was a young girl, her dad often jokingly introduced her as "My little girl, Ralph." Time after time throughout her childhood Christina was embarrassed and, yes, more than a little irritated when her father teased her like that. After all, girls aren't named Ralph. Now—at last—Christina had sweet revenge. This was her turn to tease her dad. She named the little runt "Ralph" so for all the years to come, her dad would hear the name "Ralph" in the house thousands and thousands and thousands of times.

Ralph had no idea where he was, who these "Mom" and "Dad" people were, or what was going on. All he knew was

The Real-Life Story of Crazy Ralph

that he had to get busy exploring. "Enough of this Christmas present chit-chat," Ralph thought, "I gotta take a look around."

While Christina was busy explaining why she decided to get Mom and Dad a puppy for Christmas and why she chose "Ralph" for his name, Ralph saw his opportunity. Everyone was distracted. He leaped from Dad's lap. Off he was . . . his little legs already in full-speed-ahead mode before even hitting the floor. Mom & Dad and Christina all tried to retrieve him as he scurried under the kitchen table, then behind a curtain covering the sliding glass door that opened to the outside.

The curtain draped down to the floor so all that could be seen were his little white-tipped paws sticking out underneath the curtain bottom. But they weren't his front paws. They were his back paws that were sticking out. Ralph wasn't really hiding behind the curtain. He was looking out the door glass with his front paws high up on the glass. There was a big animal out there. A huge 4-legged creature with a scraggly little tree growing out of its head! "WOW! What in the world is that???"

Ralph was looking out at Mom & Dad's backyard. That would be the backyard Ralph would be seeing pretty much every day for the rest of his life. This was his new home. His permanent home. And Christina's parents were now his human mom and dad.

And what was the huge creature with the tree branches growing out the top of its head, you ask? That was a male deer with big antlers . . . often called a "buck." Ralph's new home had a small patch of woods behind it and deer roamed through them most every day, usually stopping for a meal of corn and sunflower seeds that Mom & Dad put out for them in a feeder at the edge of the woods.

Deer were just the beginning of all the new things that Ralph would be discovering. And his new human mom and dad would be with him on many of his discoveries . . . for the rest of his life.

He had so much to see and he was so anxious to see it all. Ralph was in a permanent state of excitement. He was charging ahead on his great adventure. He just couldn't wait to begin exploring his new home and the outside world that surrounded it. Ralph had no idea where his explorations would take him.

CHAPTER 10
It's the simple things

Ralph's human dad & mom tried to contain little Ralph in their kitchen area. Two doors, in addition to the sliding glass door to the backyard, could be closed to keep him in there.

They set up a soft-sided kennel with a comfy bed inside, then placed it in a corner of the kitchen with a water dish just outside the kennel door which was always kept open. They fed him the best dog food they could find. But Ralph wasn't that all interested in drinking and eating and sleeping. He was most keenly interested in, you guessed it, exploring and adventuring.

He started by tasting the things around him, just to see what those things were made of. First came the legs of the wooden stools sitting next to the kitchen counter. He chewed on them—each of them—and discovered that they were like a tree branch he'd found outside at the animal shelter. They were wood, yes, and it was quite fun in Ralph's estimation just to feel the texture of the wood on his tongue and be able to gradually whittle them down to a bunch of toothpick-sized splinters. His teeth were amazing, he thought.

"What a tool!" Ralph exclaimed to himself, "and they're always right in my mouth ready to go to work whenever I need 'em."

Ralph then moved on to the base of the wooden kitchen table, chewing bits off here and there just to find out what it was made of and, yes, to continue testing his recently discovered teeth.

He already knew what fabric was. He laid on a cloth blanket, a fabric, many times. But now he found out what drapes were made of, curtains they're sometimes called, that covered the big glass sliding door in the kitchen. Over the course of the next few days, he chewed on them until they became frayed so badly that they had to be taken down and thrown away.

Ralph just couldn't stop exploring, tasting, and inspecting. Even when he was confined to the kitchen.

He enjoyed getting outside more than anything. He would softly whine—it sounded more like an "eek"—whenever he had to go potty. It wasn't long before Ralph learned that he was able to go outside whenever he "eeked." No, he didn't really have to go potty most of the time that he "eeked." He just wanted to be in that huge outdoor world. He loved it! He had eyes to see, ears to hear, a nose to smell, a snout to rub things, legs to carry him, and teeth to grab stuff and chew it. "What more could a guy want?" Ralph thought. He could do almost anything his mind could think up.

It's the simple things

It was wintertime in Minnesota now and Dad had plowed a big pile of snow in the backyard right outside the porch. Cold as it was Ralph wanted to be outside. All by himself was just fine. He wanted to explore everything outside even though the snow was so high above his head that he couldn't see anything at his ground level. So he would sit atop the big snow pile and just watch all the squirrels and deer and bunnies. This was his television, so to speak. And entertained he was.

The snow pile was so cold that Ralph really didn't sit on it—he held his butt about an inch above it. And he would shiver and shiver. But he didn't want to come in. He just loved being out in the big world. What a host of wonderfully different critters there were. Some were on the ground. Some in the trees. Some even flying in the air!

Ralph came to love the snow. Once when he was older and bigger, Mom let him outside immediately after a big snowstorm. The snow was so deep and Ralph ran so fast that all you could see was a flurry of snow like a powerful white tornado tearing around the lawn. That was Ralph in the center of that swirling tornado, but you couldn't even see him. It was a thrill to watch. But that was much later . . . when he grew up.

Ralph would sniff and chew on most anything he could find. And he would dig in the snow here and there and everywhere to find things—twigs, acorns, maybe a lawn sprinkler that Dad had forgetfully left out and was now buried in the snow.

No leashes or ropes were necessary to keep Ralph in the outside lawn and the adjoining woods. It was still winter and he was too small to crawl very far through the heavy snow. And there was always plenty to explore and to watch. Ralph would sit atop his snow mound off and on throughout the day shivering while intently watching all the critters and observing the amazing things they could do. He was studying their every movement. He was coming to know everything each animal did and how they did it. Years later, as Mom & Dad thought back on these times, they came to believe that Ralph's studying these various animals and their ways—when he was so very young and impressionable—caused him to think that he could do the same things. Bolt and run like a deer. Take hugely long hops like a rabbit. Run straight up and straight down trees like a squirrel. Even fly like birds and hawks. In Ralph's mind, Mom and Dad came to think, he believed he could do it all, too, when he grew up.

As winter turned to spring and the snow began to melt, Ralph was overjoyed. You see, he didn't realize that there were seasons: winter, spring, summer, and fall. All he had seen so far was winter around his new Minnesota home. Imagine his joy when the snow melted and green grass began to pop up—grass like he had seen at the animal shelter where he lived briefly. The trees had magnificent green leaves all over them. All fun to chew on and taste. And he always loved dandelions since he grabbed that winter-wilted one at the animal shelter.

Mud was especially fun. To Ralph, it felt good just getting his paws covered in the stuff. But Ralph never did anything in a small way. Even with his ventures into the world of mud . . . as you'll shortly see.

CHAPTER 11
Ralph grows into "Crazy Ralph"

It's important that those reading this story understand what "crazy" means, at least as it's applied to Ralph. And which, ultimately, became part of his name, "Crazy Ralph."

"Crazy" doesn't necessarily mean anything bad. It simply means that the individual so labeled (in this case a dog) does outrageous, over-the-top things . . . things most of us would never even consider doing. For instance . . .

The Great Muddy Mole Hunt

One day when Ralph was about 5 months old—still very much a puppy—he was introduced to a new animal he'd never seen before. You wouldn't expect Ralph to have seen one before because this animal lives underground. It's called a mole. And it burrows along in the earth just below the grass surface searching for worms, grubs, beetles, and other bugs.

That's what moles eat. Moles push up the grass from below as they search for food. And their "runs" (the path where they've been burrowing, pushing up the grass as they go) can ruin a nice lawn. So Dad was constantly trying to remove them from the yard.

Dad was particularly irritated with a mole that had single-handedly destroyed one section of the yard. This mole's runs were everywhere, crisscrossing each other, running side by side. This part of the lawn was a mess and Dad couldn't seem to trap him. So, out of frustration, Dad put the garden hose into a recently burrowed run and turned the water on. Ralph watched with great anticipation. Dad and Ralph figured they knew right where he was. So Dad began digging there. Ralph dug, too. Furiously they dug until the hole was wider and wider, deeper and deeper. The hose was running the whole time so everything got very muddy . . . including, most notably, Dad and Ralph. Especially Ralph.

Ralph and Dad had created a large muddy hole in the lawn, about 3 feet in diameter and 2 feet deep, with all their digging. Suddenly, Ralph stopped digging and stared down into the muddy waters. Then he thrust his head deep down into the waters with a splash, emerging a split-second later with a squealing mole in his mouth . . . both dripping with mud. Ralph stepped back from the hole and put him down in the grass. He'd never seen such a strange-looking creature. The mole tried to escape by digging a hole and burrowing under the grass again. Ralph watched intently. Then quickly, but gently, Ralph grabbed him with his mouth before he could disappear below the earth again. Ralph started to carry him around, the mole squealing the whole time. He would put him down and watch the mole struggle to escape, then pick him up again. He wanted to see how he worked ... like a child would watch a toy and try to figure it out. He would toss the mole up in the air, then bring him back to Dad to show him his prize. Then put him down again and the mole would commence trying to escape again.

Ralph's playing with the mole went on for about 10 minutes. Never once did he hurt the mole. He was just "adventuring" and the mole probably sensed that.

Even though Dad and Ralph ruined a healthy-sized section of the lawn trying to find the mole and spent hours doing it, they decided to let it go. It was a mutual agreement between Dad and Ralph. Ralph picked the mole up one last time and walked behind dad to the woods where they released him. The mole quickly dug into the soft earth and disappeared.

Just how Ralph knew where the mole was—where to stick his head in the muddy waters to grab him—we'll never know.

Dad and Ralph spent the rest of the afternoon filling the hole with dirt and cleaning themselves up. They really hadn't accomplished much. But it was quite an adventure for Ralph. And it was foretelling. Ralph caught many animals during his life but never hurt one.

It wasn't long after the "catch-and-release" mole hunt that Ralph ventured into landscaping, probably more aptly described as "de-landscaping." Dad was removing the weeds and thistles from the edge of the backyard with the intent of laying down sod, thus enlarging the yard. Dad couldn't seem to remove a little three-inch diameter tree. It was an oak. Their roots are especially strong and grow very deep. As much as Dad tugged and pulled, it wouldn't let go. He dug around the base of the tree, deeper and deeper. Ralph was watching closely. He followed behind Dad's heels as Dad twisted the tree round 'n round trying to break it loose from its roots. No luck.

Dad went into the house to make a phone call, then about 30 minutes later walked to the shed to get an ax. The only option to remove the little tree would be to chop it down. As he walked out of the shed, ax in hand, Ralph appeared with the tough little tree—roots and all—gripped firmly in his mouth. He was walking toward Dad, staggering from side to side a bit because the tree was around 6 feet tall with its heavy root ball still attached. The expression of "Victory!" on Ralph's face was priceless. He looked up at Dad as he lowered it to the ground as if to say, "So where would you like this?"

How did Ralph pull up that tree . . . roots and all? Who knows. Probably he was mimicking what Dad was doing when he twisted and pulled on the tree and dug around the roots. Ralph was always very observant which became abundantly clear as time went on.

CHAPTER 12
Runs like a deer, climbs like a squirrel

As you now know, Ralph wasn't just "watching" the deer and squirrels and bunnies and birds when he was a little puppy in the backyard. He was studying them. He studied their every move for hours on end. Ralph came to think that he could do anything they could. And without really thinking about it, he imitated their ways.

For instance, he ran like a deer—not just lightning fast, but he actually ran like a deer. He would bolt off with the thrust of a rocket being launched. Then he'd run the way deer and horses do when they want to go super fast. Like a high-speed gallop. No other dog that his human mom and dad had ever seen ran the way Ralph did. No other was even close to as fast. It was a treat to watch. And as you might have guessed, Ralph only had one speed . . . full-on, pedal-to-the-metal, breakneck speed.

When Ralph took off, you didn't want to be standing behind him—his paws dug deep into the lawn and threw up tufts of grass and dirt and the occasional earthworm as he blasted off. By the time the earthy debris landed, you could no longer see Ralph. He was already out of sight.

Probably the best example of Ralph's taking on other animals' ways was his tree climbing. Ralph would run furiously after a squirrel, beginning with the famous Ralph "blast-off" and a flurry of grass tufts launched towards the sky behind him. The squirrel would escape up a big tree. Ralph would run up the tree right behind him. Seriously, Ralph would be climbing the tree using the momentum of the speed he'd attained by the time he reached the tree. So he would usually climb up the tree a good 6 to 8 feet before he fell back to the ground with a thud. Falling never deterred him from chasing after the next squirrel that came across his path. He apparently felt that practice would make perfect . . . that the next time he would be successful. He never stopped trying.

It should be made clear that Ralph's love of squirrel chasing didn't mean that his intent was to harm them. No, he was simply engaged in a friendly bout of skills. He had outrun countless squirrels while they were on the ground. And never even tried to harm one. But he couldn't seem to master their tree-climbing skills. Just why he never stopped trying baffled Mom & Dad. You'd think after dozens of failed attempts that Ralph would give up. Did he know that one day something would change—somehow—that would allow him to climb trees? That sounds a little far-fetched but it seems that Ralph knew more than humans did in some ways.

Runs like a deer, climbs like a squirrel

Ralph's "I-can-do-anything-squirrels-can-do" attitude got him into very serious trouble while visiting the cabin of a family friend in southern Minnesota. The cabin sat next to a dried-up creek bed with a very steep rock cliff on the other side of the creek. The cliff was almost straight up about 30 to 40 feet high (picture the length of 3 or 4 cars stacked up end to end, bumper to bumper). The rock wall had a few clumps of grass and weeds sticking out here and there but it was almost totally rocks along its face.

While Mom and Dad stood on the cabin side of the dried-up creek visiting with their friend, Ralph was allowed to run free—after all, they were out in the country with nothing but grass and weeds and trees around. No cars. No way Ralph could get into trouble. Yeah, right.

Ralph ran into the woods beside the cabin. When he hadn't returned and wasn't heard from in about 15 minutes, Dad and Mom started to get a little concerned. Dad called out loudly, "Ralph, come here." Mom called out, too. But still no Ralph. Suddenly, a few pebbles tumbled down from atop the rock cliff into the dried-up creek bed below. Then a few more pebbles. Then some small rocks came tumbling down the wall. Mom, Dad, and their friend looked up to the top of the rock wall cliff. Ralph was on the edge looking down on them. Ralph, evidently, was thinking that he could walk down the wall like a squirrel walks down a tree. Truth be told, a squirrel would probably never attempt a climb down this rock wall. But that didn't deter Ralph.

The Real-Life Story of Crazy Ralph

Whether Ralph started to climb down the side of this nearly sheer rock wall—almost straight up & down—or if he accidentally started to slide off the edge is not known. What is known is that Ralph had all 4 legs locked on "full-brake" and was coming down. There was no stopping anything now. All Mom and Dad and their friend could do was watch in horror.

The flow of little rocks down the cliffside increased, followed by bigger rocks and sand, then the mass of rocks and weeds and debris became larger. Ralph was right behind all of it. His speed increased rapidly. It was a fall, no doubt, but controlled somewhat by Ralph's braking and occasional running. Yes running! As Ralph's rate of descent increased and he got closer to the cliff bottom, he stopped braking and put his legs into full-speed run mode. His legs were running as fast as he was falling. By the time he hit the dried creek bed at the bottom of the cliff, Ralph's legs were moving so fast that they were almost a blur. He landed with such muscle-driven leg power that he launched himself across the full width of the creek bed when he hit ground level. It was a sight to be seen. Unbelievable! Ralph miraculously came through that combination fall/run without injury. For people who hadn't witnessed this themselves, the incident as described would be far-fetched. Preposterous!

The expression on Ralph's face on the way down wasn't fear . . . or confusion . . . or terror . . . or anything else like what you'd expect. It was an expression of pure excitement. This was, to Ralph, just another part of the great adventure he was on. The risk of serious injury or even death didn't seem to make any difference to him. "What a wonderful world, what a great place," Ralph thought. "I love cliffs!"

The car ride home was uneventful. Mom and Dad talked about the cliff incident all the way while Ralph slept soundly in the back. They were certain they would never see anything like that again and that Ralph could never do anything crazier.

Of course, they were wrong. Very wrong.

CHAPTER 13
I can fly!

It was a bright sunny spring day in April as Dad drove home from the store with Ralph in the back seat. Ralph was now about 3 or 4 years old. They were listening to Elvis on the radio. Ralph would occasionally burst out with a howl—sounding just like Elvis, or so he thought. Ralph loved music and preferred it to be played loud. The louder the better. He especially liked the fast rock 'n roll tunes. As you can now probably better understand, Ralph just didn't sit back and listen to the music. He was **IN** the music. He would howl along, jump and pace to the rhythm, and occasionally let out a powerful, thunderous bark that would have knocked Elvis flat on his back.

Dad reduced the radio volume and put the rear window down so that Ralph could share his beautiful howling voice with the world. Truth is, Dad was trying to reduce the howling volume inside the car. They were only a half-mile away from home now on a quiet neighborhood street. Ralph stopped "singing" and poked his head out the window. He loved the breeze that flopped his ears and all the odors that wafted by at 20 miles per hour. Car rides were, like most all things, his favorite.

They arrived home and Dad shut off the radio and rolled up Ralph's window. He couldn't see Ralph. "He must be lying down on the back floor," Dad thought to himself. He shut the car off, got out, walked around to the back door, then opened it expecting Ralph to leap out like a huge frog as he usually did. But there was no Ralph! The back seat area was empty. He wasn't in the car! Where could he possibly be?? The only answer to Ralph's disappearance was that he'd jumped out the window . . . someplace along the last half-mile or so when Dad opened Ralph's back window fully. But they were traveling 20 miles per hour or better! Ralph could be killed, seriously injured at a minimum it would seem.

Dad jumped back into the car and drove quickly down the same street where he first opened Ralph's window, then started hollering as loud as he could, "Ralph, come here! Come here, boy!" He didn't see Ralph anywhere along the street or in the street. So he must have survived. Maybe he crawled under a bush or into someone's garage? He was probably hurt badly. Just think what would happen to you—any living creature, really—if you jumped out of a car moving at 20 miles per hour on a blacktop road. You could hit your head and suffer a brain injury, or you could easily break your arms or legs or shoulders or worse.

Frantic now, Dad turned the car around and slowly drove back towards home looking between garages and houses and

I can fly!

around trees and bushes. Maybe Ralph was hurt and trying to limp home or was lying in pain beneath someone's picnic table. God only knows. Just then, Dad spotted Ralph running down the sidewalk toward home. He wasn't crawling or limping or even whimpering. Ralph spotted Dad and ran towards the car. He jumped right in the back seat as Dad opened the door. Ralph looked all but perfect! Yes, his fur was dusty and dirty (he must've rolled around in the street a few times after jumping out the window) and the underside of his chin was raw. So he most likely did a Ralph-launch out the window, then hit the street on his front paws and the underside of his chin.

The look in Ralph's eyes was simply excitement as Dad tried to scold him for doing something so dangerous. Thereafter, Ralph's window was only rolled down part of the way—just enough to get his head out. Ralph probably would've jumped out of an airplane window if the opportunity ever arose. Birds can fly, you know.

CHAPTER 14

Daring escapes—how did he do it?

As you now know, Ralph was a consummate escape artist. He could get out of just about anything. And away from just about anybody who had him on a leash.

His leash-escape method was simple but effective. Normally, Ralph would be straining and pulling at the leash as someone walked him. But walker beware should the leash suddenly slacken. Because that would almost certainly mean Ralph was preparing to do his "power-launch" escape. He would leap with full-thrust power using his very strong rear legs. The slack would instantly be taken up. This powerful yank on the leash would startle the walker and throw him or her off-balance. Ralph would follow through with full-speed run mode, pulling the walker down to the ground . . . usually resulting in the walker losing their grip on the leash. Thus, Ralph would be off on another adventure.

This power-launch followed by a full-speed run may seem

The Real-Life Story of Crazy Ralph

like a harmless enough escape method. But not really. The walker usually ended up with skinned knees and/or palms and/or elbows as he or she fell to the pavement. Mom's brother, Bill, wound up with serious cuts and bruises from being pulled into the brick wall of the garage. He had to be taken to the emergency room for stitches. Bill had been warned of Ralph's leash-escaping ways but, as Bill later said, "I was unprepared for how quickly it happened. As we went out the service door of the garage, Ralph walked around the corner and immediately did his power surge pulling me into the corner of the brick garage. My face and mouth got the worst of it."

Of course, Ralph would never intentionally hurt anyone. He just never looked back at the damage he had done.

There were many such episodes. Probably the most injurious one was when a good friend, "Wim" from The Netherlands in Europe, decided to take him for a walk one wintry day. Wim and his wife had been staying with Mom and Dad for a week or two. Wim was a very large man—he weighed over 250 pounds—and was not afraid of anything or anybody. We warned him about Ralph and the damage that he had done to others who tried to walk him. Wim couldn't be dissuaded. He loved all animals and had come to especially love Ralph. "No one can pull me down, certainly not a 40-pound dog," Wim said as he opened the front door and walked Ralph down the sidewalk. They had just reached the blacktop driveway when Ralph did his power-surge escape maneuver. He pulled this powerful 250-pound man to the ground with a shattering thud. Wim's left shoulder hit hard—very hard—on the blacktop. His shoulder was seriously injured and had to be operated on when he returned home to the Netherlands. Not even a 250-pound man holding the leash was a match for Ralph at the other end.

It was one of these daring daytime escapes that resulted in a criminal record for Ralph. Or, you could say, a career opportunity.

CHAPTER 15
Ralph becomes a police dog—briefly

Dad was taking Ralph out for a walk one beautiful summer day. Well aware of Ralph's escaping ways—and having suffered more than a few falls gaining this awareness—Dad gripped the leash firmly and stayed on high alert. After 5 or 10 minutes of walking around the yard, Dad lowered his guard briefly to look at the squirrels robbing the bird feeder of their sunflower seeds. Dad was distracted. Ever vigilant for such an opportunity, Ralph walked back towards Dad, the leash slackened, and Ralph bolted. Dad tried to hang on but his legs got tangled as he tried to turn in Ralph's direction . . . and he fell, releasing the leash as he did. Ralph was off on another adventure.

Over the years, it became Ralph's practice to return home after a short time of "adventuring." So Dad and Mom waited. And waited and waited. But Ralph didn't return. Something must be wrong. Dad and Mom got in their car and began searching the neighborhood, gradually moving their search

The Real-Life Story of Crazy Ralph

out farther and farther away from their house. Occasionally, they'd return to the house to see if Ralph had come home on his own. But no Ralph. It was worrisome. Had he been hit by a car and maybe was lying by the side of the road somewhere? Had he strayed into a yard with big dogs and they attacked him?

Finally, after several hours of increasingly frantic searching, Mom called the police to report Ralph's disappearance. "Yes, we picked up your dog Ralph a while ago and he's in lockup now at the local animal shelter," Mom was told by a police officer. Mom and Dad rushed over to the shelter to meet with another police officer who could go inside the lockup and retrieve Ralph. The police officer was waiting in his police car outside the animal shelter when Mom and Dad arrived.

"I picked Ralph up not far from your home a few hours ago," said the officer, "but I didn't know where he lived so I drove around with him in the back of my police car to see if I could find someone out searching for him." Mom & Dad had forgotten to put Ralph's new dog license on his collar. A serious mistake which, as it turns out, they were later fined for.

The policeman and Ralph instantly became fast friends. Ralph stuck his nose out between the bars on the back window enjoying the breeze and the changing smells as they drove. The policeman told him to look for the house where he lived. After over an hour of searching and thoroughly enjoying each other's company, the policeman had to take Ralph to the animal shelter so he could get back to real police work.

Ralph becomes a police dog—briefly

"He was a great companion," the policeman told Mom and Dad as they stood outside the animal shelter. "I would love to have him as my partner to patrol with me every day."

The policeman then went inside the locked animal shelter and retrieved Ralph with a leash. When Ralph came out and saw Mom and Dad, his face lit up and he started to strain on the leash to meet them. Mom and Dad thought they might be witnessing the policeman about to be pulled to the ground with a Ralph "blast-off." But just then the policeman and Ralph passed the police car parked with its door open. Ralph turned quickly and tried to jump back in. He wanted to go riding around with the policeman again! Maybe he had decided he wanted to be a police dog, what's called a K-9. He certainly would love riding around all day and chasing criminals!

Mom and Dad loaded him up in their car and took him back home where he belonged. And so ended Ralph's ever-so-brief career as a rookie K-9 police dog.

But Ralph was shortly going to meet something more exciting to chase around than plain ol' criminals.

CHAPTER 16

Look what I found, Dad! Can I keep him . . . please, pleeease?

Early one summer morning when Ralph was close to four years old, Dad took him along on a ride to pick up some car parts from a friend who lived in the country. The friend's home was just a 45-minute drive south of where Dad and Mom and Ralph lived.

The ride was uneventful except for Ralph's back & forth pacing in the back seat—first to look out one window, then immediately turning around and going back to look out the other window. Ralph didn't want to miss seeing anything. He was always on full alert to see new things and learn new things. Of course, that's the stuff adventures are made of. Nothing passed by Ralph unnoticed.

Now maybe Ralph spotted something new and exciting along the way, perhaps something very close to their destination. Dad didn't know. But as soon as they arrived, and as

Dad went to put Ralph's leash on, Ralph bolted "full-steam" out the opened car door and was instantly off in a cloud of dust. His paws were a blur digging deep into the gravel driveway for traction as he accelerated. He reached full speed by the end of the friend's driveway, leaped across the country road, then disappeared in the high weeds. He was headed in the direction that they'd come from. Yes, he must've seen something on the way.

Dad went running after him. There was a farm house just down the road a few blocks that they had passed by—the only building in sight—so Dad headed there. A white fence stretched all around a grass field with a barn inside the fence at one corner. Dad heard something like rumbling thunder as he got closer to the fenced-in field. The thunder had kind of a rhythm to it. Just then a huge horse came galloping by on the inside of the fence. With each gallop, his hoofs hit the ground with a resounding thud. It was this stream of thuds coming in rapid succession as the horse ran that made the thunderous sound.

Why in the world was a horse running so fast in this fenced field? Was he simply entertaining himself? Was he afraid of something? Was he chasing something?

Just then, wouldn't you know it, a streak of black and white fur came running by. It was Ralph! Crazy Ralph! He was chasing the horse and was only a few feet behind him. Dad watched in horror not knowing if the horse would give Ralph a powerful kick in the head. Or maybe turn around and run over him.

Look what I found, Dad! Can I keep him . . . please, pleeease?

Ralph continued to chase the horse round and round the field—one direction, then the other direction. It was a hot day and both Ralph and the horse had to be getting tired.

Finally, the horse ran into the barn . . . probably out of desperation. Ralph ran in right behind him, hot on his trail. Dad climbed the fence and rushed toward the barn door. Dad had to stop this madness before Ralph got seriously hurt, maybe even killed.

Just then, the horse came galloping out of the barn with Ralph right on his heels. Dad dove for Ralph with both hands, grabbing him around the chest, then getting a grip on his collar. It was over. Ralph was panting hard. Very hard. His tongue was hanging full out. Dad never realized how very long his tongue was. It was smattered with dirt and straw. Ralph was clearly exhausted but not ready to quit the chase. Not by any means. Dad held on hard. Ralph looked straight up at Dad, his big dark brown eyes brimming over with wild excitement. Dad knew exactly what those eyes were saying, "Look what I found, Dad!! Just look at this thing!! Have you ever seen anything like it? Can I keep him . . . PLEASE, PLEASE, **PLEEEEASE?**"

It must have been absolutely thrilling for Ralph to see a horse for the first time. And right up close.

Cindy, the lady who owned the horse, witnessed the chase from her living room window. Surprisingly, she wasn't upset at Ralph's high-speed pursuit of her horse. She explained to Dad that her horse wasn't really afraid of Ralph—he was playing with him. Had the horse felt truly threatened, Cindy said, he would've kicked Ralph—who was running right on his heels—smack dab in his head. The result would've been one of two things: Ralph would either be dead (the likelihood) or would have suffered such pain that he would never chase a horse again.

Ralph was so tuckered out that he slept in the back seat all the way home. Another first-of-its-kind adventure. Another memory he could live over and over again in his dreams.

Ralph loved life and life loved him. Most every adventure he took himself on—somehow—turned out just fine. But something was about to walk into his life that would change everything. It all began innocently enough with a conversation between Mom and her niece, Lynny.

CHAPTER 17

Can you take the little guy in? Would it be OK with Ralph?

In the spring of 2004 when Ralph was about 3½ years old, Mom and Dad attended a family Easter gathering . . . brothers and sisters, aunts and uncles, nephews and nieces, grandpas and grandmas. It was quite a crowd. Ralph stayed home.

Dad's niece, Lynny, spotted Mom in the back yard of the house where the gathering was being held and approached her with a question. Lynny was obviously distraught. The backstory was simple enough but the question was a little more complicated.

Lynny explained to Mom (her aunt) that she had brought a dog home from the animal shelter to live with her. It was a small male dog, under 10 pounds, a mixed breed of (probably) Chihuahua & Rat Terrier. After staying just a few days at Lynny's townhouse, it became clear to Lynny that she couldn't keep him. The little dog, named Squirt, chewed on everything

he could get his mouth around, peed wherever and whenever he felt like it; and on top of everything else, wasn't very friendly. So he simply couldn't stay at Lynny's townhouse. BUT she didn't want to take him back to the animal shelter where she got him because she feared he would be "euthanized." You see, because he had the behavioral problems he did, he couldn't readily be adopted into another home, so he would likely be put to sleep. Euthanized. Animal shelters don't keep dogs indefinitely, especially problem dogs like Squirt.

"Is there any way you could keep him at your house?" Lynny asked Mom. "Could you take him? Could you give him a home?" Mom could see how painful it was for Lynny knowing that her only other option was to return him to the shelter which would probably be his last stop in life's journey. Mom said, "Yes, he can come and live with Dad and I . . . oh . . . and with Crazy Ralph, of course."

Lynny was elated. A great burden was lifted from her shoulders. The little guy would not have to go back to the shelter. He would have a new home with people who could care for him. Later on Lynny went to find Dad, her uncle, among the party guests. He was in the house talking with his brother. She broke into the conversation with a loud "Thank you so much!" and gave Dad a huge hug.

Of course, Dad had no idea why he was being thanked and hugged so hard. But Lynny quickly explained her little dog dilemma and how Mom (who was still in the back yard) had just agreed to take him home. Then Lynny went happily off to tell her parents about the little dog's new home. She was

The Real-Life Story of Crazy Ralph

thrilled! But Dad was a little baffled. This was the first he had heard that she even had a dog. And, apparently, it was already agreed that he'd be living at his house.

A few minutes later, Mom came into the house and up to Dad—not knowing that Lynny had already talked with him. She proceeded to tell Dad the little dog story and how Lynny asked if he could live with them. She then said, "What do you think we should do . . . we need to tell Lynny yes or no?" Mom pretended that Dad would have to agree before a decision would be made. She failed to tell him that she'd already agreed to take the little guy into their home.

Dad appeared to be thinking the issue over deeply. A frown appeared on his brow as he pondered. Not a word was said. Mom rushed to fill the silence with all the reasons that Squirt should move in. Maybe she should've been honest in the first place and told him that she had already made the decision. But it was too late now.

Mom hastened to point out that Squirt would make a good companion for Ralph, that it was just as easy to take care of two dogs as one, the house was certainly big enough, visits to dog parks would be even more fun . . . and on and on until she couldn't think of any more reasons why Squirt should become part of their family. Finally, feeling defeated, she looked down and began to speak.

"I should tell you something," Mom said sheepishly, "I've already told . . ." Dad interrupted her with a huge smile on his face. "Oh, no I'm the one that has something to tell you—I've already talked to Lynny and agreed that Squirt should come live with us." Mom was greatly relieved and Dad had had his fun. They hugged. Both Mom and Dad were thrilled to have another dog come to live with them.

Arrangements were made for Lynny to bring the little guy over to Mom and Dad's house the next day. Of course, it was Ralph's house, too. And there was a real concern that Ralph would not want another dog in his house. You see, many dogs—maybe most—are "territorial." That is, they don't want other dogs coming into *their* homes and being with *their* humans. Hopefully, Ralph wouldn't be territorial. Ralph was much, much larger—over 4 times heavier and probably 3 times taller–so he would be the boss of the little guy for sure.

Of course, like everything else with Ralph, nothing went as expected. The little dog's introduction to this new home was, well, let's just say . . . eventful.

CHAPTER 18

Get outa my way, you big fur bag!

As planned, Lynny brought the little guy to Mom and Dad's house the next morning right at 10 o'clock. She knocked at the front door. Ralph stood up straight and started barking loud enough to startle everyone in the house . . . and everyone in all the other houses around them. Ralph's favorite was other people coming to visit. Everything, as you now well know, was Ralph's favorite. His world was full of favorite things to do, favorite people to meet, favorite foods to eat, favorite everythings.

Ralph was delighted when he saw Lynny and the little dog she was carrying. A new playmate, Ralph was thinking, as he jumped up and down, back and forth and side to side. Yes, Ralph was excited. Lynny put the dog down on the floor and announced, "This is 'Squirt.'" Not a very fearsome name, perhaps, but quite fitting. He had short little legs, a white body with large brown spots and short hair. He was a cutie. But a cutie with an attitude.

The Real-Life Story of Crazy Ralph

Now . . . Mom was the one who took care of Ralph from the beginning. Bathed him. Fed him. Trained him (or tried to). She was all but Ralph's full-time companion. Dad was usually away at work. And now she would be doing the same for Squirt.

Ralph stopped jumping long enough to greet the newcomer, putting his nose right up to Squirt's. Ralph's tale was whizzing back and forth. He was excited, he was happy, and he wanted to play. Ralph's introduction was met with a growl and a baring of the teeth from Squirt. He didn't like Ralph. Actually, he didn't seem to care much for anybody—Mom, Dad, not even Lynny. He walked into the kitchen and started to inspect, sniffing Ralph's blanket, then Ralph's chewie toy . . . growling and snarling each time Ralph approached. He wanted no part of Ralph.

Lynny left. The front door closed. The atmosphere was tense. Nobody knew quite what to do. Ralph tried repeatedly to make friends with Squirt but to no avail.

The days that followed weren't much different. As time passed, Ralph approached Squirt to make friends less and less often. Ralph's advances were always met by mean snarls and occasional nips, not quite biting Ralph but letting him know that he should stay his distance. Pretty soon Ralph stopped trying to make friends altogether.

At mealtimes, Mom would fill both dogs' bowls at the same time. Squirt would quickly finish eating his bowl full of food, admittedly a much smaller bowl but proportionate to his petite size. Then he would come over to Ralph's bowl and try to eat

Ralph's food, nudging Ralph's snout out of the bowl altogether. Ralph was so good-natured. He didn't even try to fight for his food. He was much, much bigger than Squirt and could easily have put out Squirt's lights with one chomp on his little head. But he never even growled at him. He simply started ignoring Squirt and his selfish ways.

There were many such selfish incidents. For example, Squirt would notice that Ralph was busy chewing on his favorite rawhide bone. Squirt would tug on it harder and harder until Ralph let go. Same thing if Ralph was playing with a toy. Or playing chase-the-ball with Dad. Squirt was the living definition of the word, "irritation."

Now just when things started turning around, no one knows. But gradually—very gradually—Squirt began to calm down the meanness stuff. He started to lose his "I-don't-want-anything-to-do-with-you" attitude. Ralph didn't seem to care. Now Ralph didn't want anything to do with Squirt. Ralph had had enough of Squirt's attitude. That's the way it seemed anyway.

Then one cold fall day, Mom noticed Ralph laying down in a sunbeam pouring through the living room window. Ralph loved the warmth of the sun on his fur as he lay on the soft carpeting. Yes, you guessed it: sunbeams were Ralph's favorite. Another favorite in a never-ending list of favorites. Squirt would typically do the same but at another window. But today was different. Squirt came over and plopped himself down near Ralph—not close to him, but near. Ralph noticed but didn't move. The next time Mom looked, Squirt was a little

The Real-Life Story of Crazy Ralph

closer to Ralph. Then a bit later, he was closer yet. "Amazing," Mom thought.

In the weeks to come, Ralph and Squirt started playing together. More and more. They were gradually and most certainly becoming friends. Good friends. They both seemed to be enjoying life more than ever. Ralph looked forward to greeting Squirt every morning with a nudge of his snout, then a lick on the face. Yes, they had become buddies.

They both would sleep with Mom & Dad at night. Squirt would have to run from across the room to get enough momentum to spring-leap onto the bed. Ralph just crouched at the edge of the bed, then effortlessly—almost in slow motion—leaped on. Squirt would nuzzle his way under the covers. Ralph would lay down on top of the covers right next to the "Squirt lump." They slept together every night. Squirt under the blankets, Ralph on top. But always right next to each other.

One of the games Ralph liked to play was "Toss the Squirt." It worked like this. Ralph would sneak up on Squirt. Then, before Squirt realized what was going on, Ralph would thrust his snout under Squirt's belly and launch Squirt high into the air with an upward thrust of his snout. Squirt would land on the carpeting—usually feet first—and then chase Ralph all around the house.

Squirt's game of choice was "Sneaky Snatch." In this game, Squirt would sneak attack Ralph from behind as Ralph laid on his stomach chewing one of his toys. Squirt would nip at one of Ralph's rear ankles causing Ralph to immediately look behind him at his nipped ankle. Squirt would quickly dash around the opposite way that Ralph was looking and snatch the toy away from him. Then he would drop it nearby so they could play the Sneaky Snatch game again.

Crazy Ralph and his little buddy, Squirt. Each enriched the other's life. They grew to do everything together. They ate, slept, played, ran away, "sunbeam-bathed," visited dog parks, traveled, and as you might expect, got into trouble together. Everything. But Ralph now assumed the leadership role. And, not a big surprise, taught Squirt all of his crazy ways.

CHAPTER 19
Double trouble

One warm summer day, Mom & Dad drove Ralph & Squirt to a nearby dog park. Both dogs loved dog parks. Ralph especially. They could both run free. As usual, Ralph got so excited as they neared the park that he could hardly contain himself. He loved to meet and play with other dogs . . . the more, the merrier. Mom took Squirt into the fenced-in park on his leash, Dad took Ralph in on his leash.

Once inside the gate, Ralph strained so hard on the leash that he almost pulled Dad over. Dad released him and he leaped into the short weeds along the path they were on. He immediately lifted his leg and began to pee. But he lowered his bottom and also began to poop. Both at the same time . . . while starting to run! A lady entering the dog park with her friend and their dogs excitedly pointed at Ralph and exclaimed, "Look at that dog! He's pooping and peeing at the same time! And he's running, too!! I've never seen anything like that!!" No one had ever seen a dog do that before. Ralph simply couldn't waste any dog-park time.

Then Ralph immediately tore off down the path and around the little pond where other dogs were gathered. Squirt tried the same bathroom trick that Ralph just performed but it simply didn't work for him. Finally, he lowered his lifted leg and raised his bottom—defeated at accomplishing Ralph's dual-potty trick—and tore off, too. Squirt often mimicked Ralph but it never seemed to work quite the same for him.

Within 60 seconds of Ralph's tearing down the path, something occurred that could only be called an "explosion." Ralph never slowed down as he reached the cluster of dogs which, as it turns out, were involved in a group training lesson with their humans—learning to "Sit," "Roll over," that sort of thing.

The result was genuinely explosive. Ralph literally crashed their training party. He put on the brakes and skidded into the center of the group knocking a few dogs to the side in the process. Then all the dogs scattered wildly. They didn't know what that black & white tornado was that just hit them!

In truth, Ralph's explosive entry was simply his way of inviting everyone to one wild party.

All the dogs immediately started running—first after Ralph, then each other in the most frenzied play that their dog owners had ever witnessed. Yelping, barking, creating a dust storm all around them. The swarm of dogs then moved into the pond as Ralph guided them on his tour of pure, full-on mayhem.

The dogs were now all in and around the water, splashing and running back and forth. A sight to behold. But not a sight appreciated by the dog owners who were now themselves in a frenzy trying to catch their dogs, leashes in hand.

As dog owners were chasing down their dogs and loudly calling out their names, Ralph suddenly stopped to take a drink from the pond. Within seconds, all of the dogs calmed down and also started taking a much-needed drink from the pond. The dog owners stared in amazement. Who was this Ralph dog that had such amazing power over all the other dogs? What in the world just happened? They were in disbelief, amused, upset, and shocked—all at once.

Mom and Dad decided to leave before everyone came down from their shock. Dad quickly hooked Ralph on his leash and they took off down the path back to the car with Mom waving her goodbyes to the dazed onlookers. And Squirt? He had been beside Ralph the whole time. His little "Yip" was barely audible in all the craziness but he never stopped yipping and running and churning everyone up the whole time. Squirt was still partying even after Ralph and all the other dogs stopped to take a drink.

As Dad and Mom and Ralph hurriedly left, Squirt raced after them . . . his little legs kicking up mud and dirt, his face filled with joy and pride and excitement. There wasn't any question—Squirt was proud to be Ralph's buddy. In truth, Squirt had now become Ralph's little brother. And that brotherly bond only grew stronger as time went on.

CHAPTER 20

Two years of living crammed into each year of life

It can truthfully be said that Ralph experienced at least twice as much during his life than most dogs. Probably more like three or four times as much. Ralph simply never slowed down, never quit. And Squirt was always nearby struggling to keep up.

There was the time when an unleashed Ralph caught a rabbit while visiting a family friend's lake cabin. Yes, Ralph was that fast. He proudly presented the limp rabbit to Mom & Dad, gently laying it down by their feet. "Look what I caught!" his eyes seemed to say. The rabbit didn't move. Dad couldn't believe that Ralph would kill a rabbit—really, any living creature. But there was no doubt that the rabbit was dead. Dad looked the rabbit over closely. It wasn't injured in any way. Evidently, it had simply died of fright which is not unusual for rabbits when cornered by predators.

The Real-Life Story of Crazy Ralph

Ralph's eyes now seemed to say, "Oh what have I done." He went over and laid down next to the nearby shed. Ralph never just laid down, especially in the middle of the day and most especially when he was outside and unleashed. But Ralph was in mourning. It took some time for Ralph to become Ralph again.

Then there was the day that a visitor to Mom and Dad's house didn't shut the front door tightly and Ralph escaped with Squirt right behind him. This happened not long after Squirt came to live with Mom, Dad, and Ralph . . . so Squirt wasn't very familiar with the outside surroundings. And he hadn't fully bonded with the family yet.

Off Ralph was on one of his adventures, disappearing into the patch of woods that surrounded the house. Squirt couldn't keep up but, like Ralph, also disappeared into the woods. In about a half hour, Ralph returned home. But there was no Squirt. Mom and Dad searched frantically for the little guy but he was nowhere to be found. So they put Ralph on a leash and simply went wherever Ralph led them. About a half-mile away they spotted Squirt heading in the opposite direction of their house. Ralph had led them right to Squirt.

Maybe Squirt didn't have the same sense of direction as Ralph did. It was like he was lost. Maybe looking for something. He was walking fast but not running. Mom and Dad tried to catch Squirt so they could carry him back home. But Squirt wasn't having any of it. He would dart away every time Mom or Dad approached. Just where he was going and why, Mom and Dad didn't know. But Squirt was determined. And

Two years of living crammed into each year of life

there was no way he was going to let himself get caught. The four of them—Mom, Dad, Ralph, and Squirt—were now over a mile away from home.

Dad sensed that Ralph somehow understood the situation. So he let Ralph off his leash. Ralph and Squirt had not yet become fast friends at the time—as they later would be—but Ralph nonetheless was about to take the lead in getting Squirt back home to safety. What Ralph did next was nothing short of amazing.

First, Ralph positioned himself right beside Squirt and walked at the same pace. Then, he pulled in front of Squirt and gradually began to turn around towards home. All Squirt could see was Ralph's behind and his big paws. Squirt followed Ralph like that all the way home and right back into the front door. This "Follow Me" episode would be repeated time and time again over the years whenever Squirt was afraid. Squirt would simply stay very close to Ralph and go wherever Ralph was going. Ralph gradually became Squirt's big brother, always ready to protect him, always ready to lead him to safety.

Ralph took his self-assigned protective duties quite seriously. Even in his most adventurous quest, Squirt's safety was always on his mind. He would never let harm come to his little buddy. It was easy to see. Ralph was—in every sense of the word—Squirt's full-time bodyguard.

One day Mom & Dad took Ralph and Squirt to a huge dog park. Ralph and Squirt had become fast friends by this time. The park was about 80 acres large and there were always dozens of dogs at play. Ralph loved it. Squirt, on the other hand,

The Real-Life Story of Crazy Ralph

was apprehensive—he felt anxious, wary. On this day, Squirt stood next to Mom and Dad while Ralph went off on an adventure with a half-dozen new dog friends running with him. All of them were quite large dogs.

Other dogs were always attracted to Ralph. Every place Ralph went there was a party. He would burst into a run and all the dogs around would tear off with him. Ralph loved the swampy area in this dog park with all of its towering green grasses . . . and, yes, mud. Lots of mud. You couldn't see Ralph for all the tall grasses and swamp reeds but you could hear him and his half-dozen dog entourage sloshing through the muddy waters joyously yipping all the way.

Periodically, Ralph would circle back to check on Squirt. Then he'd go off on another wild romp through the park. One time he came back to find two large dogs standing right in front of Squirt, glaring at him. Mom & Dad gently pulled Squirt back but, each time they moved a few feet back, the two big dogs would move close again. One of them snarled at Squirt. The other showed his teeth. Something was about to happen and it didn't look like it would be good.

Then something did happen. Suddenly, Ralph appeared out of nowhere coming at full speed. He wasn't slowing down. He braked at the last second with all 4 paws digging into the dirt, skidding directly into the three-dog crowd in a cloud of dust—somehow stopping precisely between Squirt and the two big dogs. Ralph stood tall. Very tall. Taller than Mom or Dad had ever seen him. His lower half was sprinkled with mud, his whole body was wet from the swamp. He had a piece of swamp grass draped over his back. And now he was being covered with that cloud of dust that he had churned up as he came to his screeching halt. Ralph was quite the sight.

He turned to face the two menacing dogs and stared right into their eyes. Ralph's backend bumped into Squirt as he turned. Squirt backed up a bit to make room but stayed squarely behind Ralph. The two big dogs did the same—they continued to face Ralph but they backed away a bit. There was little question what Ralph's eyes were saying to the canine bullies that had been threatening Squirt just moments ago: "You want him . . . you'll have to come through me." It was a tense moment. No one knew what would happen next.

Casually—so as not to hint that it might be scared—one of the two big dogs turned his head and started to slowly walk the other way. The other big dog decided it would be best if he moved on, too.

Squirt moved up beside Ralph as both of the big dogs turned their heads to look back. Now Squirt was standing right beside Ralph's front legs, his height not much taller than Ralph's knees. Squirt stared intently at the bullies. Fear had left his body. It was clear what his eyes were saying to the bullies: "You better get outa here before you get hurt, you mangy furballs."

It was all over. Mom and Dad were relieved. It could've ended badly. But Ralph saved the day (and Squirt's butt!).

Mom and Dad were so intent on watching the confrontation between Ralph and the bully dogs, they hadn't even noticed that a crowd of dogs had loosely formed around them a safe distance away. The nearby dogs had witnessed everything.

The Real-Life Story of Crazy Ralph

When the bullies were gone, they all came closer. Several gently nudged little Squirt, others came up to Ralph, who was now sitting, and crouched down playfully. Still, others just walked up to Ralph and looked admiringly into his eyes, then moved on. They all were congratulating Ralph and telling him how proud they were to have met him. And it seemed that they all envied Squirt for having someone like Ralph as a big brother.

Mom & Dad, Ralph & Squirt all went home with an even stronger bond between them. And to celebrate their special day, they stopped at the Dairy Queen where they all had their favorite ice cream cone treat. Squirt cuddled up next to Ralph in the back seat for the ride home. What a day.

There were a number of instances when Ralph stood tall for Squirt over the years. If Squirt needed his help—even if Ralph was busy adventuring—Ralph would stop dead in his tracks to come to Squirt's aid. A short "Yip" from Squirt was all it took for Ralph to come running. Ralph served as Squirt's protector all of his life. It was obvious to Mom and Dad that Ralph saw his bodyguard role as his single most important duty in life.

Squirt and Ralph now did everything together. They even napped together. Ralph would lay on his side, Squirt would snuggle up to his tummy and lay down . . . so they could feel each other's warmth and breathing and heartbeats. They were one. Ralph now fully assumed his role of big brother. He would determine when and where they would nap. Same with bedtime. Squirt would wait until Ralph went up the stairs to Mom and Dad's bed.

CHAPTER 21
It all came on unexpectedly

Exactly when Ralph started to get sick, Mom and Dad were not sure. Sometime late in the year 2008. The sickness came on suddenly. Mom and Dad tried everything to get him better—special foods, medicines, interesting toys to play with, new dog parks to visit. But nothing seemed to help. They took him to his veterinarian several times but even she couldn't figure out what was wrong with him. The most she could determine was that it was probably a brain issue.

All Squirt could do was watch as Ralph got sicker. Ralph no longer took notice when Squirt approached him from behind ready to nip his ankle. It used to be their favorite game and Ralph had always been ready to play. No more. Ralph didn't "snout-toss" Squirt any longer either, despite all kinds of encouragement from Squirt.

There was little fun left in anything for Ralph, it seemed.

By Christmas 2008, Ralph was very sick. He was now over 8 years old and was not getting any better. He started going to the bathroom on the carpeting, doors, even the TV stand. Ralph never did that in all his years. Never. It was obvious that he couldn't help himself. He could no longer think clearly. Occasionally, he would howl loudly. Or give out a shrill, high-pitched whine . . . then a seizure. He was in pain. And the pain wouldn't go away.

Mom and Dad took Ralph to the vet once more. He had always loved seeing her, wagging his tail furiously when she came in the examination room, licking her hand, looking up at her with his big sparkling brown eyes. But now Ralph's eyes were dull, his head was lowered. The vet examined him again. Ralph couldn't even muster up enough energy to wag his tail a bit.

After taking X-rays and blood samples, the vet came back into the room. The vet said that Ralph probably had some kind of brain injury or brain disease that was not curable. But she really wasn't sure. All that could be done is wait and watch. Maybe, by some miracle, Ralph could overcome and recover.

CHAPTER 22

The adventure of all adventures! The grandest of them all!!

Ralph wasn't howling and whining much anymore. His eyes were distant. He was listless. It was now February 2009 and Dad was going out of town the next day. So he decided to first take Ralph to his favorite dog park and let him run. Maybe the fresh air would help. Maybe just being with other dogs, chasing each other, sniffing things and such would perk him up.

Ralph didn't get excited and jump all over in the car as they neared the park . . . like he always had in the past. Sadly, he threw up in the back seat during the drive. He was sick. Very sick. They spent only about 15 minutes walking in the park. Ralph had no interest in anything, not even the other dogs.

Dad went out of town the next day as planned. Ralph got worse. It became clear that there was probably no life-saving miracle on the horizon for Ralph.

The Real-Life Story of Crazy Ralph

Late the next day, Ralph came to Mom. He was trembling. He looked into Mom's eyes. His eyes were pleading. Mom could tell what his eyes were saying: "Please help me." It was late at night. Mom loaded him up in the car and took him to a special veterinarian clinic that's open 24 hours. Ralph walked in slowly. He was all but completely drained of energy.

They laid Ralph down and made him comfortable. Mom rubbed his paw gently. She wondered how many miles Ralph had put on his paws over the years. They sure got a workout.

Ralph closed his eyes and began to breathe slowly. He started dreaming about his mother who he hadn't seen since he was her "little runt" . . . now so long ago. He'd always missed her, always thought about her. Now he could almost feel her. Smell her. Hear her.

Yes, yes, he **could** see her! Her blurry image became clearer and clearer. And that was her scent, no doubt. She was now perfectly clear and standing right there beside where he was laying. He could feel her mouth gently pulling him up by the back of his neck, his scruff—just like she did when he was first born and couldn't even see yet.

"Mother . . . it is you!"

It was at that very moment that Ralph died. He had departed this world. He was in another place now. He had left his old worn out, sick body behind.

He leaped up and touched his mother's nose with his. He breathed in her wonderful scent. There was no more pain.

The adventure of all adventures! The grandest of them all!!

Everything in his body was like new. Ralph was Ralph again. He was overjoyed beyond description!

For the longest time, Ralph and his mother just licked each other and rubbed each other with their noses. They were both overjoyed.

Ralph then looked around. What a bowl-'em-over wonderful place, he thought. Lush green pastures and huge trees. Dogs of every make and model nearby—chasing butterflies, racing after each other, playing games. There were bubbling streams, huge waterfalls, meandering rivers, and Lilly ponds to drink from and splash around in. And there was that magnificent warm sun that he'd always loved from his first trip outside the animal shelter now so long ago.

Ralph could see caves and mountains off in the distance. And lakes and oceans. And islands and peninsulas. And . . . and . . . and. There was an endless number of places to explore and countless, exciting things to experience. He saw horses and cows and moles . . . every kind of critter imaginable. There were many kinds of animals that Ralph had never even seen before.

Of particular interest was the little bridge just on the horizon. It was made up of every color in the rainbow. Ralph wondered what was on the other side of it. Yup, there was no end to the wonderful adventures he could go on and the friends he could take with him. He was about to go adventuring like never before.

Indeed, **this** was—truly was—the grand adventure that Ralph had been seeking all his life on earth.

The Real-Life Story of Crazy Ralph

Some people call dying "passing away." That means passing into another world. You see, dying doesn't really mean "dead." The body can die, everyone's body will die someday, but the person inside it doesn't die. They just pass on into another world—truly a paradise that we call heaven—where they're made young and healthy again.

So do dogs go to heaven, you ask? Absolutely. But it's thought that they first go to a place called Rainbow Bridge where they live until their human mom or dad also dies and comes for them. Then they walk together across that most brightly colored bridge into heaven. Ralph was now in that wonderful place just outside heaven called Rainbow Bridge.

So how do we know dogs will go to heaven? Simple. God has promised all of us humans that heaven has everything to make us perfectly happy. Everything. "You will not want for anything," God's son Jesus said in describing heaven. Many of us could not be perfectly happy without our pets that became such an important part of our family on earth. So, by God's proclamation spoken through Jesus—by virtue of how he defined heaven, that is it's everything you could ever want—the pet you so love will most assuredly be with you in heaven one day.

When you think about it, God would not make such loving and lovable creatures like dogs and cats for you to hold close to your heart on earth and then just toss them away leaving you with a hole in your heart for all eternity. True love is the greatest gift that God gave to all of the creatures he created. And love doesn't just go away.

And if you and your family are another religion? Not a Christian?

No matter. Most all religions—Christianity, Judaism, Hinduism, Islam, etc.—believe in a life after the one we're in. Likewise, most all religions believe dogs will be there. Probably the best summary on the subject (which also has references where you can read more about pets going to their new life) can be found on the Internet.* Here's the bottom line of their studies:

> "Nearly every major religion throughout the world does believe that dogs go to heaven after they die. Some are more clear than others, but there is a consensus that pets go to heaven or some kind of paradise after death."

Ralph's dog mother now lived in heaven with her human family. She had come back across Rainbow Bridge to welcome Ralph home. She told Ralph—her special "little runt"—that she was going back across the bridge into heaven but would come to visit him every day. They would lay close together in the sun on the soft, lush-green grass and tell each other all

---

* https://farewellpet.com/where-do-dogs-go-after-death-beliefs-of-different-religions/

about what they'd done while on earth. For now, Ralph could embark on his adventuring. "Do whatever you want," she said, "play, explore, run free anywhere with anyone. Heck, poke your head into the clouds if you like. Or . . . well . . . maybe you should just look behind you." Then, with a huge smile on her face, she turned to leave.

Ralph looked behind him. He immediately lit up with excitement. Yup, there was a wily squirrel running up a big tree. Another squirrel wasn't far behind. You guessed it. Ralph gave chase. As he approached the tree at full speed, he leaped up and started climbing . . . expecting to quickly tumble down, as he always did. He'd done this very same thing hundreds of times on earth and never could get very high up on the tree. Maybe 6 or 8 feet before crashing down with a thud. It never stopped him from trying again and again, most anytime he spotted a squirrel.

But now things were wonderfully—incredibly—different. Ralph ran straight up the tree and sat down on a big branch right next to the squirrels. He did it! He finally did it!! It goes without saying that Ralph was thrilled to the core. And the squirrels felt the same. They loved the chase and never felt threatened by Ralph. You see, animals in this wonderful place don't have any desire to hurt or even fear other animals anymore.

Ralph was loving it.

On top of all else, he took great comfort in knowing that one day he would be with his human mom and dad again. His dog mother had told him so. "Just wait. Wait outside heaven's

The adventure of all adventures! The grandest of them all!!

gate where you are now, Rainbow Bridge. And enjoy everything knowing that one day they'll be with you again." What about Squirt, Ralph thought. "Oh, he'll be here with you one day, too," his mother told him, "so will your brothers and sisters." Ralph was now content just knowing his heaven would be complete one day, filled with all the love he's ever known.

Yes, the place he was now in was called Rainbow Bridge, the area named for the bridge connecting it to heaven.

Ralph was bubbling over with all the things he could do while he waited for his human mom and dad and brothers and sisters. But, before adventuring any more, he thought he should introduce himself to the other dogs nearby. As he was about to take his first step, a Golden Retriever ran past him with such speed that the rush of wind almost knocked him over.

"That guy is *really* fast," Ralph thought as he struggled to catch up to him. Suddenly the beautiful young Golden Retriever stopped and turned his head to greet Ralph who was now coming up beside him. Ralph told him how impressed he was to see such speed, "Wow, you're faster than a bolt of lightning," Ralph said, "Yup . . . lightning speed . . . **lightning** . . . hey, THAT'S IT, I know you!! **You ARE 'Lightning'**. I met you at the animal shelter back when I was a puppy and you were really old. Do you remember?"

The Golden Retriever remembered him well. Turns out, Lightning had to be put in the shelter because his human dad was in the hospital for a long time and there was no one else to take care of him. Surprisingly, his dad gradually got better. But by the time he came to get his beloved dog at the shelter, Lightning had passed away.

Ralph recalled how he had laughed to himself about the name "Lightning" because the ol' Golden Retriever hardly ever so much as moved back then. That was cruel to even think, Ralph realized, and he apologized to Lightning for being disrespectful even though it was just a thought in his mind back then. Lightning explained to Ralph how depressed he was at the time—not knowing if he'd ever see his human dad again.

Then a black Cocker Spaniel came running up to them. This Spaniel was the very definition of joyfulness. He was in the highest of high spirits. Ralph instantly took to him. He just radiated happiness.

The adventure of all adventures! The grandest of them all!!

"Ralph, I want you to meet my good friend Happy," Lightning said. Then it hit Ralph like a ton of those concrete blocks that lined the walls at the animal shelter. This was the dog who paced back & forth in his kennel during Ralph's animal shelter days. Happy didn't look at all happy back then. Like Lightning, he too was seriously depressed at the time. His human mom and dad needed nursing care and had to move into a small apartment. They couldn't take him with them. Happy died within a week after Ralph left the shelter with Christina. Ralph apologized to Happy, too, for making fun of him back then . . . even though it was just in his mind.

All three dogs—Lightning, Happy, and Ralph—agreed that they couldn't be more pleased with how things turned out. They were all now in the most indescribably wonderful place in all the heavenly universe.

Suddenly Lightning froze, his eyes locked on a figure off in the distance. Lightning's body began to quiver. His tail started to whip back and forth, faster and faster . . . 'till it became almost a blur. Then he leaped forward running at top speed off into the distance. Ralph could see that the figure walking their way was a human, a man. The man started walking faster and faster toward Lightning, then he too started running. It was Lightning's human dad that had loved Lightning so much for all of their years together on earth.

Their reunion was the most joyous thing Ralph had ever witnessed. The man and his life-long companion were hugging and kissing and petting. Tears of absolute joy filled both their eyes. After giving Lightning one last belly rub, the man stood up and started walking across the Rainbow Bridge into heaven with Lightning beside him. Lightning looked back at Ralph and Happy and, through the joyful tears that filled his eyes, said, "I'll come back to visit whenever I can." Lightning and his dad would now live together forever in heaven.

Ralph witnessed the same kind of joyous reunions many times after that. He knew his day would come. And now that he knew what heaven was—everything you love will be with you—he knew for sure that his little buddy Squirt would be with him one day, too, along with his dog mother and all his dog brothers and sisters. And, of course, his human mom and dad.

Ralph thought—if he could say something to the family he left on earth—it would simply be this: "Please be happy for me. I can't wait to be with you again. In the meantime, I hope you will bring another dog into your home and give him such a wonderful life as I had with you. Oh, and as for you Squirt, get ready for an into-the-clouds snout toss when you get up here, little buddy."

Ralph had finally found what he'd been seeking all his life: The adventure of all adventures. This was it. Being in the overwhelmingly beautiful Rainbow Bridge with an infinite number of "crazy" fun things to do.

Life in Rainbow Bridge—
The Very Grandest Of Grand Adventures

The adventure of all adventures! The grandest of them all!!

And, of course, this is Ralph's absolute favorite of all favorites. Forever.

Can Ralph's greatest adventure—doing most everything and anything he likes in Rainbow Bridge—be topped by other dogs? No. **BUT** it can absolutely be equaled by every other much-loved dog and other pet around the world. Yours, too. And Ralph will be there to greet him or her when they come. You can bet on it.

Epilogue

Squirt mourned Ralph's passing for a very long time. He would repeatedly search every room of the house for Ralph, sniff the carpeting and couches where Ralph used to lay, look for Ralph's food bowl and water dish . . . he simply couldn't understand what happened to him. Squirt was seriously depressed for weeks. There was little lust for life left in him. And try as Mom and Dad may, there was no way to explain to him where Ralph was.

But something quite interesting began to happen as Squirt gradually came out of his depression. He began to act like Ralph. Do some of the same "crazy" things Ralph did. Go at things with unbridled "gusto" like Ralph always did. Squirt was even seen "snout-tossing" a little stuffed pony that Mom and Dad kept at their house for their granddaughter to play with.

Yes, Squirt was taught well. He was becoming a mini-Ralph. . . which was no small undertaking. But that's a whole 'nother story.

We trust that Squirt will see Ralph again one day and that they can again sleep in their sunbeam together and go adventuring together.

The Rainbow Bridge

Just this side of heaven is a place called Rainbow Bridge.

When an animal dies that has been especially close to someone here, that pet goes to Rainbow Bridge. There are meadows and hills for all of our special friends so they can run and play together. There is plenty of food, water and sunshine, and our friends are warm and comfortable.

All the animals who had been ill and old are restored to health and vigor. Those who were hurt or maimed are made whole and strong again, just as we remember them in our dreams of days and times gone by. The animals are happy and content, except for one small thing; they each miss someone very special to them, who had to be left behind.

The Rainbow Bridge

They all run and play together, but the day comes when one suddenly stops and looks into the distance. His bright eyes are intent. His eager body quivers. Suddenly he begins to run from the group, flying over the green grass, his legs carrying him faster and faster.

You have been spotted, and when you and your special friend finally meet, you cling together in joyous reunion, never to be parted again. The happy kisses rain upon your face; your hands again caress the beloved head, and you look once more into the trusting eyes of your pet, so long gone from your life but never absent from your heart.

Then you cross Rainbow Bridge together into Heaven. . . .

Author Unknown
(RainbowBridge.com)

Dedication

Dedicated to my grandchildren, Danny, Emma, and Aubrey, who were the inspiration for this book. They always wanted to hear a bedtime story about "Crazy Ralph" even though they had never met him. And I never tired of telling his stories. Still don't.

Boppa Harmon

Acknowledgments

Dmitry Gitelman—Initial cover design & illustrations.

Grandma "Manga" Harmon—Proofreading, editing & substantive changes without which this book would not make sense nor be readable.

Paul Nylander—Cover redesign, formatting & typesetting, and whose guidance made this book a reality.

www.ingramcontent.com/pod-product-compliance
Lightning Source LLC
LaVergne TN
LVHW021714080426
835510LV00010B/989